LIBERTY FOR ALL?
1820–1860

STUDENT STUDY GUIDE

OXFORD
UNIVERSITY PRESS

OXFORD
UNIVERSITY PRESS

Oxford University Press, Inc., publishes works that
further Oxford University's objective of excellence
in research, scholarship, and education.

Oxford New York
Auckland   Cape Town   Dar es Salaam   Hong Kong   Karachi
Kuala Lumpur   Madrid   Melbourne   Mexico City   Nairobi
New Delhi   Shanghai   Taipei   Toronto

With offices in
Argentina   Austria   Brazil   Chile   Czech Republic   France   Greece
Guatemala   Hungary   Italy   Japan Poland   Portugal   Singapore
South Korea   Switzerland   Thailand   Turkey   Ukraine   Vietnam

ISBN 978-0-19-522320-0 (California edition)   ISBN 978-0-19-518884-4

Writer: Kent Krause
Project Manager: Matt Fisher
Project Director: Jacqueline A. Ball
Education Consultant: Diane L. Brooks, Ed.D.
Design: designlabnyc

Casper Grathwohl, Publisher

9 8 7 6 5

Printed in the United States of America
on acid-free paper

Dear Parents, Guardians, and Students:

This study guide has been created to increase student enjoyment and understanding of
A History of US.

The study guide offers a wide variety of interactive exercises to support every chapter. At
the back of the guide are actiivity maps to help tie your study of history to the study of
geography. Also, you will find several copies of a library/media center research log to use
to organize your time researching proejcts and assignments. Parents or other family
members can participate in activities marked "With a Parent or Partner." Adults can help
in other ways, too. One important way is to encourage students to create and use a
history journal as they work through the exercises in the guide. The journal can simply be
an off-the-shelf notebook or three-ring binder used only for this purpose. Some students
might like to customize their journals with markers, colored paper, drawings, or
computer graphics. No matter what it looks like, a journal is a student's very own place to
organize thoughts, practice writing, and make notes on important information. It will
serve as a personal report of ongoing progress that your child's teacher can evaluate
regularly. When completed, it will be a source of satisfaction and accomplishment for
your child.

Sincerely,

Casper Grathwohl
Publisher

This book belongs to:

_____

CONTENTS

HOW TO USE THE
STUDENT STUDY GUIDES TO
A HISTORY OF US

One word describes A History of US: stories. Every book in this series is packed with stories about people who built a brand new country like none before. You will meet presidents and politicians, artists and inventors, ordinary people who did amazing things and had wonderful adventures. The best part is that all the stories are true. All the people are real.

As you read this book, you can enjoy the stories while you build valuable thinking and writing skills. The book will help you pass important tests. The sample pages below show special features in all the History of US books. Take a look!

Before you read

- Have a notebook or extra paper and a pen handy to make a history journal. A dictionary and thesaurus will help you too.

- Read the chapter title and predict what you will learn from the chapter. Note that often the author often adds humor to her titles with plays on words or **puns**, as in this title.

- Study all maps, photos, and their captions closely. The captions often contain important information you won't find in the text.

27 Howe Billy Wished France Wouldn't Join In

A **hoop-stay** was part of the stiffening in a skirt; a **jupon** was part of a corset. **Matrons** are married women. The **misses** are single girls; **swains** and **beaux** are young men or boyfriends. **Making love** meant flirting. **British Grenadiers** are part of the royal household's infantry.

General Howe had already served in America. In 1759 he led Wolfe's troops to seize Quebec.

Sir William Howe (who was sometimes called Billy Howe) was in charge of all the British forces in America. It was Howe who drove the American army from Long Island to Manhattan. Then he chased it across another river to New Jersey. And, after that, he forced George Washington to flee on—to Pennsylvania. It looked as if it was all over for the rebels. In New Jersey, some 3,000 Americans took an oath of allegiance to the king. But Washington got lucky again. The Europeans didn't like to fight in cold weather.

Sir William settled in New York City for the winter season. Howe thought Washington and his army were done for and could be

Swarming with Beaux

Rebecca Franks was the daughter of a wealthy Philadelphia merchant. Her father was the king's agent in Pennsylvania, and the family were Loyalists. Rebecca visited New York when it was occupied by the British. Her main interest in the war was that it meant New York was full of handsome officers:

My Dear Abby, By the by, few New York ladies know how to entertain company in their own houses unless they introduce the card tables....I don't know a woman or girl that can chat above half an hour, and that on the form of a cap, the colour of a ribbon or the set of a hoop-stay or jupon....Here, you enter a room with a formal set curtsey and after the how do's, 'tis a fine, or a bad day, and those trifling nothings are finish'd, all's a dead calm till the cards are introduced, when you see pleasure dancing in the eyes of all the matrons....The misses, if they have a favorite swain, frequently decline playing for the pleasure of making love....Yesterday the Grenadiers had a race at the Flatlands, and in the afternoon this house swarm'd with beaux and some very smart ones. How the girls wou'd have envy'd me cou'd they have peep'd and seen how I was surrounded.

126

6

As you read

- Keep a list of questions.

- Note the bold-faced definitions in the margins. They tell you the meanings of important words and terms – ones you may not know.

- Look up other unfamiliar words in a dictionary.

- Note other sidebars or special features. They contain additional information for your enjoyment and to build your understanding. Often sidebars and features contain quotations from primary source documents such as a diary or letter, like this one. Sometimes the primary source item is a cartoon or picture.

After you read

- Compare what you have learned with what you thought you would learn before you began the chapter.

The next two pages have models of graphic organizers. You will need these to do the activities for each chapter on the pages after that. Go back to the book as often as you need to.

finished off in springtime. Besides, Billy Howe loved partying. And some people say he liked the Americans and didn't approve of George III's politics. For reasons that no one is quite sure of, General Howe just took it easy.

But George Washington was no quitter. On Christmas Eve of 1776, in bitter cold, Washington got the Massachusetts fishermen to ferry his men across the Delaware River from Pennsylvania back to New Jersey. The river was clogged with huge chunks of ice. You had to be crazy, or coolly courageous, to go out into that dangerous water. The Hessians, on the other side—at Trenton, New Jersey— were so sure Washington wouldn't cross in such bad weather that they didn't patrol the river. Washington took them by complete surprise.

A week later, Washington left a few men to tend his campfires and fool the enemy. He quietly marched his army to Prince-ton, New Jersey, where he surprised and beat a British force. People in New Jersey forgot the oaths they had sworn to the king. They were Patriots again.

Those weren't big victories that Washington had won, but they certainly helped American morale. And American morale needed help. It still didn't seem as if the colonies had a chance. After all, Great Britain had the most feared army in the world. It was amazing that a group of small colonies would even attempt to fight the powerful British empire. When a large English army (9,500 men and 138 cannons) headed south from Canada in June 1777, many observers thought the rebellion would soon be over.

The army was led by one of Britain's

The Road to Saratoga

▮ ROUTES TAKEN BY BRITISH

▮ ROUTES PLANNED BY BURGOYNE

☆ BATTLE

General Burgoyne's redcoats carried far too much equipment. Each man's boots alone weighed 12 pounds. They took two months to cover 40 miles from Fort Ticonderoga to Saratoga, and lost hundreds of men to American snipers.

127

GRAPHIC ORGANIZERS

As you read and study history, geography, and the social sciences, you'll start to collect a lot of information. Using a graphic organizer is one way to make information clearer and easier to understand. You can choose from different types of organizers, depending on the information.

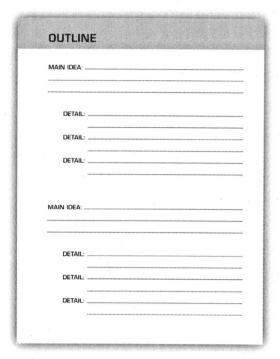

Outline

To build an outline, first identify your main idea. Write this at the top. Then, in the lines below, list the details that support the main idea. Keep adding main ideas and details as you need to.

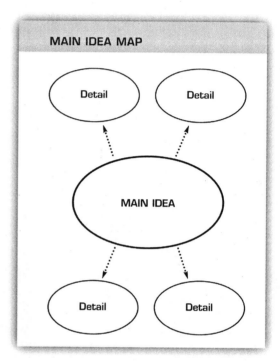

Main Idea Map

Write down your main idea in the central circle. Write details in the connecting circles.

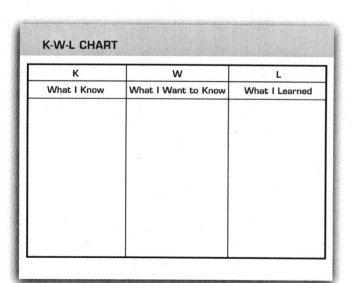

K-W-L Chart

Before you read a chapter, write down what you already know about a subject in the left column. Then write what you want to know in the center column. Then write what you learned in the last column. You can make a two-column version of this. Write what you know in the left and what you learned after reading the chapter.

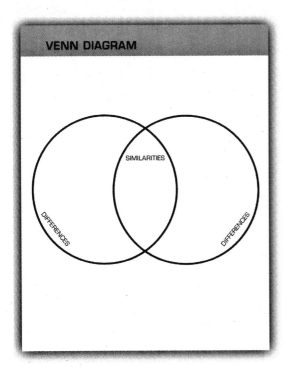

Venn Diagram

These overlapping circles show differences and similarities among topics. Each topic is shown as a circle. Any details the topics have in common go in the areas where those circles overlap. List the differences where the circles do not overlap.

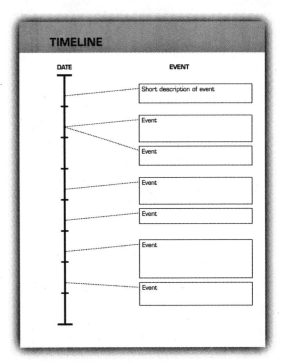

Timeline

A timeline divides a time period into equal chunks of time. Then it shows when events happened during that time. Decide how to divide up the timeline. Then write events in the boxes to the right when they happened. Connect them to the date line.

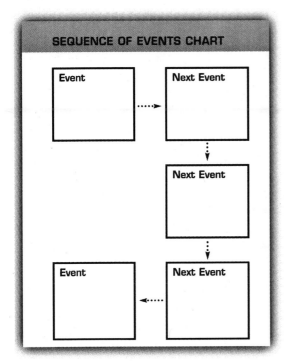

Sequence of Events Chart

Historical events bring about changes. These result in other events and changes. A sequence of events chart uses linked boxes to show how one event leads to another, and then another.

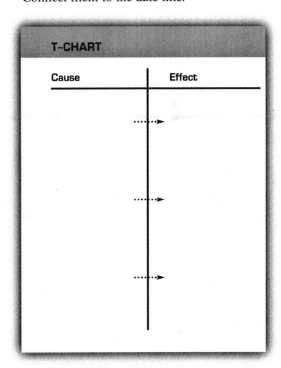

T–Chart

Use this chart to separate information into two columns. To separate causes and effects, list events, or causes, in one column. In the other column, list the change, or effect, each event brought about.

REPORTS AND SPECIAL PROJECTS

Aside from the activities in this Study Guide, your teacher may ask you to do some extra research or reading about American history on your own. Or, you might become interested in a particular story you read in *A History of US* and want to find out more. Do you know where to start?

GETTING STARTED

The back of every *History of US* book has a section called "More Books to Read." Some of these books are fiction and some are nonfiction. This list is different for each book in the series. When you want to find out more about a particular topic from the reading, these books are a great place to start—and you should be able to find all of them in your school library.

Also, if you're specifically looking for *primary sources*, you can start with the *History of US Sourcebook and Index*. This book is full of *primary sources*, words and evidence about history directly from the people who were involved. This is an excellent place to find the exact words from important speeches and documents.

DOING RESEARCH

For some of the group projects and assignments in this course, you will need to conduct research either in a library or online. When your teacher asks you to research a topic, remember the following tips:

TO FIND GOOD EVIDENCE, START WITH GOOD SOURCES

Usually, your teacher will expect you to support your research with *primary sources*. Remember that a primary source for an event comes from someone who was there when the event took place. The best evidence for projects and writing assignments always comes from *primary sources,* so if you can't seem to find any right away, keep looking.

ASK THE LIBRARIAN

Librarians are amazing people who can help you find just about anything in the library. If you can't seem to find what you're looking for, remember to ask a librarian for help.

WHEN RESEARCHING ONLINE, STICK TO CREDIBLE WEBSITES

It can be difficult to decide which websites are credible and which are not. To be safe, stick with websites that both you and your teacher trust. There are plenty of online sources that have information you can trust to be correct, and usually they're names you already know. For example, you can trust the facts you get from places like pbs.org, census.gov, historychannel.com, and historyofus.com. In addition to free websites like these, check with your librarian to see which *databases and subscription-based websites* your school can access.

USE THE LIBRARY/MEDIA CENTER RESEARCH LOG

At the back of this study guide, you'll find several copies of a Library/Media Center Research Log. Take one with you to the library or media center, and keep track of your sources. Also, take time to decide how helpful and relevant those sources are.

OTHER RESOURCES

Your school and public library have lots of additional resources to help you with your research. These include videos, DVDs, software, and CDs.

THE LONG WAY WEST

SUMMARY *In the early nineteenth century, Americans knew little about the vast land west of the Mississippi River.*

ACCESS

The Great Plains looked much different in the early 1800s from how it looks today. To organize the information in Chapter 1, use the outline graphic organizer on page 8 of this book. While reading the chapter, identify two or more main ideas that relate to the area west of the Mississippi River (for example, "Long's Expedition" and "Opinions about the Region"). Write these down on the lines labeled "Main Idea." Then add details from the chapter about each main idea in the lines below.

WORD BANK   iron horse   Great American Desert   prickly pear

Choose words from the word bank to complete the sentences.

1. On his Map, Edwin James labeled the Great Plains the _Great American Desert_

2. Explorers found out that they could eat the _prickly pear_

3. People in the 1800s called a train an _Iron horse_

WORD PLAY   Choose two of the terms in the word bank. Write a sentence that includes both of these terms.

People in the 1800 call a train an Iron Hore and

WORKING WITH PRIMARY SOURCES   _The great plains is called The great American Deses_

Explorer Stephen H. Long wrote the following description of the region west of the Mississippi River.

> In regard to this extensive section of the country, I do not hesitate in giving the opinion, that it is almost wholly unfit for cultivation, and of course, uninhabitable by a people depending upon agriculture for their subsistence.

1. What does Long mean by "wholly unfit for cultivation?" _not Livible NOT growable_

2. Do you think Long was accurate in his assessment? Why or why not? _NO, because the land was livable_

Write your thoughts in your history journal.

WRITING

Imagine that you are part of Stephen H. Long's expedition to the Great Plains. In your history journal, write a diary entry describing a typical day of exploration.

MOUNTAIN MEN

SUMMARY *Enduring many hazards, fur traders known as mountain men took the lead in exploring the American West.*

ACCESS

Have you ever wanted to go someplace totally different from where you live – someplace more exciting? For certain people in the 1820's and 1830's, the dangerous and wild way out west was the perfect challenge. To help organize your thoughts about one of these groups of people, copy the main idea map from page 8. In the largest circle, write *Mountain Men*. In each of the smaller circles, write one important fact about mountain men that you learn as you read the chapter.

WORD BANK   rendezvous   mountain men   trekked   petrified

Choose words from the word bank to complete the sentences. One word is not used at all.

1. The *Mountain Men* traveled through Native American lands to trap and hunt furs.

2. Jim Bridger found trees that had turned to stone in a *petrified* forest.

3. Fur trappers *trekked* across the desert to reach California.

In a dictionary, look up the word you did not use. Write that word in a sentence.

TIMELINE

Copy the timeline graphic organizer on page 9 of this guide into your journal. Write 1824 at one end and 1831 at the other end. Use the map on page 18 and information from the book to put these major events of Jedediah Smith's life in the right order. When you are finished, write two adjectives that could describe Smith's life.

Smith is attacked by Paiute Indians   Mohave Indians helped his party cross the desert

Mexican officials jail Smith as a spy   Killed by Comanches on business trip

First trappers' rendezvous   Grizzly bear attack

Lives on bugs and rodents

MAP

Study the map of Jedediah Smith's expeditions on page 18. Then, using the blank U.S. relief map at the back of this guide, make your own map of his travels. Add *Jedediah Smith* to the legend and label the following cities on the map: St. Louis, Independence, San Gabriel, and San Francisco. Title the map, "Exploring the West." You will use this map for additional exercises later in the study guide.

WORKING WITH PRIMARY SOURCES

Carefully re-read the first two paragraphs on page 19, including Jed Smith's letter to his brother. In your history journal, write a few sentences about why you think Jed chose to live the way he did. Then using some of those reasons, write an ad that could appear in a newspaper in 1830, trying to attract people for a fur trapping party set to travel to the unexplored West.

RIDING THE TRAIL TO SANTA FE

SUMMARY *American merchants discovered that great profits could be made by trading in the Mexican town of Santa Fe. Hundreds of caravans traveled the trail between Missouri and Santa Fe.*

ACCESS

Do you think the end of the Santa Fe trail looked much like the beginning? In your history journal, make a two-column chart. Label one column *Missouri: beginning of the trail*, and the other *Santa Fe: end of the trail*. In each column, brainstorm and list as many descriptive words as you can about either end of the trail. Think about sights, smells, and ways of life. Use the painting on pages 24 and 25 to help imagine what Santa Fe looked like.

WORD BANK   pinnacle   rawhide   Santa Fe Trail

Choose words from the word bank to complete the sentences.

1. American merchants formed large caravans that traveled on the _Santa Fe Trail_

2. Explorers reached the _pinnacle_ of Pike's Peak in 1820.

3. Merchants carried their coins in _rawhide_ bags.

MAP

Look at the map on page 23 of your book. Answer the questions in your history journal.

1. Which two towns were at the extreme ends of the Santa Fe trail?

2. List five Indian nations that were located near the Santa Fe trail.

3. List two rivers that travelers on the Santa Fe trail had to cross.

4. What were the two different routes of the Santa Fe trail called?

On the "Exploring the West" map you began in chapter 2, add the Santa Fe trail to the legend and mark the trail on the map. Label Santa Fe and the Arkansas River.

WORKING WITH PRIMARY SOURCES

Reread the words of the editor of the *Missouri Intelligencer* on page 24. Then read the next paragraph, by 20th-century writer Paul Horgan. Suppose you are a merchant who travels with caravans over the Santa Fe trail. A relative has heard that that journey is dangerous, and asks why you continue to take such risks. In your history journal, write a letter to your relative about what it's really like to travel on the Santa Fe trail.

WRITING

You've read the author's description of Santa Fe and seen the painting on pages 24 and 25. What do you think a Southwestern town looked like in 1824? In your history journal, draw or collage a picture of a desert town in the early 1800's. Include as much as you can: animals, plants, buildings, people and landscape.

SUSAN MAGOFFIN'S DIARY

SUMMARY *Waves of American settlers, including Susan Magoffin, moved into New Mexico. These settlers helped the U.S. government gain control of the territory from Mexico.*

ACCESS

Susan Magoffin was one of only a few American women to have traveled the Santa Fe trail while Santa Fe was under Mexican control. Imagine that you could interview her. Before reading, skim through the chapter. Then in your history journal, make a list of five questions you would like to ask Susan. Read the chapter carefully and write the answers to the questions as you imagine Susan might answer them.

WORD BANK   Great Potato Famine   desolate   blight

Choose words from the word bank to complete the sentences.

1. A _Great patalo famine_ destroyed the potato crop in Ireland.

2. The _desolate_ led 1.6 million Irish to move to the United States.

3. Because it was so vast and lonely, the desert was a _blight_ place.

WITH A PARENT OR PARTNER

Look up the word blight in a dictionary. In one minute, list as many things as you can think of that can cause a blight. Ask a parent or partner to do the same. Then compare your lists.

CRITICAL THINKING   CAUSE AND EFFECT

Make a T-chart like the one on page 9 of this study guide. In the left column, write the following causes. In the right column, fill in the effects.

1. Col. Kearny captured New Mexico, so . . .

2. Susan's carriage crashed, so . . .

3. Ireland's potato crop was destroyed, so . . .

4. Susan Magoffin became ill with yellow fever, so . . .

5. Few jobs were available in China, so . . .

6. Railroad tracks reached Santa Fe, so . . .

WORKING WITH PRIMARY SOURCES   IN YOUR OWN WORDS

Susan Magoffin wrote the following words in her diary while traveling on the Santa Fe trail.

> There is such independence, so much free uncontaminated air, which impregnates the mind, the feelings, nay every thought, with purity. I breathe free without that oppression and uneasiness felt in the gossiping circles of a settled home.

In your own words, rewrite Susan's thoughts about life on the trail in your history journal.

WRITING

Have you ever felt what Susan Magoffin expressed in the passage above? Write about a time when you did.

PIONEERS: TAKING THE TRAIL WEST

SUMMARY *Seeking land and a better life, pioneers traveled west on the Oregon Trail. They faced numerous hardships on the long journey.*

ACCESS

What do you know about the pioneers who traveled west? In your history journal, copy the "K-W-L" graphic organizer on page 8. In the first column, write down anything you might know about the pioneers. Then, skim through the chapter and look at illustrations and maps. Fill in the second column with questions and things you want to know about the pioneers. As you read the chapter, make notes in the third column that answer your questions in the second column.

WORD BANK

prairie schooner   emigrant   pioneer   immigrant

Choose words from the word bank to complete the sentences.

1. My great-great-grandfather was an _immigrant_ who came from Ireland during the Great Potato Famine.

2. The _pioneers_ family packed their possessions on a _prairie schooner_ and set out on the Oregon Trail.

3. The traveler became an _emigrant_ because he had left United States territory.

WORD PLAY

Look up the word schooner in a dictionary. What are two definitions of the word that are different from how it is defined in prairie schooner? In your journal, write two sentences using the word schooner—one for each of these other definitions.

CRITICAL THINKING   MAKING INFERENCES

Chapter 5 describes in great detail the experiences of the pioneers who traveled west. Check off each of the phrases below that describe scenes that could really have happened.

___✓___ both parents in a family die from cholera three weeks after leaving Missouri

___✓___ a pioneer family travels by steamboat from Missouri to Oregon

___✓___ a baby is born under a tree

___✓___ a family buys extra furniture to carry over the Rocky Mountains

___✓___ two oxen die in the same week

___✓___ a family leaves a wagon behind at Fort Laramie

___✓___ a pioneer family travels to the West Coast in a heavy Conestoga

___✓___ Native Americans help pioneer families find water

WORKING WITH PRIMARY SOURCES

A diary tells feelings and experiences from one person's point of view. Read Amelia Stewart's diary on pages 36–37 carefully. What impressions can you form of her? Write a description of Amelia as you might imagine her on the Santa Fe Trail.

GETTING THERE

SUMMARY *Pioneers traveled west together in large wagon trains. The journey to California was made difficult by miles of desert and the rocky Sierra Mountains.*

ACCESS

This chapter describes the westward journey of a large group of pioneers. In your history journal, copy the sequence of events chart on page 9. In the first box, write "Formed a large wagon train at the jumping-off town." Fill in the other boxes with the events that followed on the wagon train's journey.

WORD BANK   wagon train   Humboldt sink

Choose words from the word bank to complete the sentences.

1. More than 1,000 pioneers traveled west with the _Wagon train_.

2. The pioneers were surprised to learn that the river disappeared under the desert at the _Humboldt Sink._

WITH A PARENT OR PARTNER

In one minute, write down as many words as you can think of that relate to a wagon train (for example, pioneer, oxen). Ask a parent or partner to do the same. Compare your lists. Use a dictionary to look up any words that either of you does not know.

CRITICAL THINKING   DRAWING CONCLUSIONS

What conclusions can you draw about some of the people in this chapter from their words and actions? In your history journal, write two or three adjectives that could describe Janette Riker, Virginia Reed, and John Bidwell.

MAP

Study the map on page 41. On the "Exploring the West" map you began in chapter 2, add the Oregon and California Trails to your legend and mark them on the map. Label the following on the map:

Oregon City   Snake River

Humboldt River   North Platte River

Missouri River.

WORKING WITH PRIMARY SOURCES

Lansford W. Hastings described the pioneers on a wagon train in 1842.

> Some were sad, while others were merry; and while the brave doubted, the timid trembled! Amid this confusion, it was suggested by our captain, that we "call a halt," and pitch our tents, for the purpose of enacting a code of laws, for the future government of the company.

Think about why the captain stopped the wagon train. Do you think the captain had a good idea? Why or why not? Answer in your history journal.

WRITING

Suppose you are traveling with a large wagon train to California. There are many disagreements among the 1,000 pioneers on this journey. The disorder and confusion seems to grow worse each day. You have been asked to write a set of laws to govern the wagon train. Ask a friend or some fellow students to brainstorm with you at least eight laws to maintain order among the pioneers.

CHAPTER 7

LATTER-DAY SAINTS

SUMMARY *Faced with persecution, thousands of Mormons trekked west to Utah. There, they built a thriving community that helped pioneers reach Oregon and California.*

ACCESS

Joseph Smith was an important religious leader in American history. In your history journal, copy the main idea map graphic organizer from page 8. In the largest circle, write "Joseph Smith" and in the smaller circles, write facts that you learn about Smith as you read the chapter.

WORD BANK

Latter-Day Saints   Mormons   utopian   polygamy   pluralism

Choose words from the word bank to complete the sentences.

1. At the time of Brigham Young's death, 140,000 _Mormons_ were living in the Utah Territory.

2. _Latter-Day Saints_ has developed in America, as evidenced in the nation's many different religious groups.

3. Joseph Smith called the members of his new religion _polygamy_.

4. In the nineteenth century, many religious groups, such as the Shakers, formed _utopian_ communities.

5. Practicing _pluralism_, or having more than one spouse, is illegal in the United States.

MAP

Study the map of the Mormon migration on page 45. On the "Exploring the West" map you began in chapter 2, add "Mormon Migration" to the legend and mark the trail on the map. Label the following cities on the map:

Palmyra   Kirkland   Nauvoo

Winter Quarters Salt Lake City.

WORKING WITH PRIMARY SOURCES

In 1844, the town of Warsaw, Illinois passed an anti-Mormon resolution:

> The adherents of Smith, as a body, should be driven . . . into Nauvoo . . . a war of extermination should be waged, to the entire destruction . . . of his adherents.

What is an *adherent*? (use a dictionary if necessary) How does this resolution violate the U.S. Constitution? Write your thoughts in your history journal.

WRITING

Imagine that the year is 1870. You are a reporter for a New York magazine who has been granted an interview with Brigham Young. In your history journal, make a list of five questions that you would ask him. One question might be "What was the biggest challenge you faced while leading the Mormons to Utah?" Next write the answers to the questions as you imagine Young might answer them.

COAST-TO-COAST DESTINY

SUMMARY *Inspired by ideas of manifest destiny, Americans, including President Polk, wanted to add California to the United States.*

ACCESS

Expanding U.S. territory from coast to coast became a very popular idea among Americans in the mid-1800s. In your history journal, copy the outline graphic organizer on page 8. While reading the chapter, identify two or more main ideas that relate to the westward movement of Americans (for example, "Manifest Destiny" and "Settling California"). Write these down on the lines labeled "Main Idea." Add details from the chapter about each main idea in the lines below.

WORD BANK   manifest destiny   rancheros

Choose words from the word bank to complete the sentences.

1. Many Americans believed it was their _____ to occupy the continent from coast to coast.

2. _____ operated large cattle ranches in California.

TIMELINE

In your history journal, copy the timeline graphic organizer on page 9. Include the following dates on your timeline: 1542, 1769, 1821, 1840, and 1846. Read the chapter to learn what happened in each of those years. Describe each event in the box next to the year in which it happened.

COMPREHENSION

In your history journal, write a sentence about each of the following people. Describe how they promoted manifest destiny.

Richard Henry Dana   James K. Polk   John L. Sullivan   Emanuel Leutze

WORKING WITH PRIMARY SOURCES

The following quote is from Ignatius Donnelly.

> Nothing less than a continent can suffice as the basis and foundation for that nation in whose destiny is involved the destiny of mankind. Let us build broad and wide those foundations: let them abut only on the everlasting seas.

1. To which continent do you think Donnelly refers?

2. To which nation do you think Donnelly refers?

3. Using your own words, describe what you think Donnelly means in the last sentence.

CHAPTER 9

A HERO OF HIS TIMES

SUMMARY *The explorations of John C. Frémont sparked great interest in California. He later helped the U.S. take control of the state.*

ACCESS

Who are some of your heroes? In the mid-1800s, John C. Frémont inspired thousands of Americans with his courageous exploits. Copy the main idea map graphic organizer from page 8. In the largest circle, write Frémont's name. In each of the smaller circles, write one fact about him that you learn as you read the chapter.

WORD BANK

longitude   topographical   Great Basin   latitude

Choose words from the word bank to complete the sentences.

1. Vertical lines on a map show _____ and horizontal lines to show _____.

2. The artist produced many beautifully illustrated _____ maps, which showed mountains and plains.

3. John Frémont traveled through Nevada and Utah, an area he called the _____.

WORD PLAY

Use a dictionary to learn the meaning of the suffix –graphy. Make a list of five words that end with –graphy. Find the definitions of these words in a dictionary. In your history journal, write sentences using each of the words on your list.

MAP

Read carefully the description of the Great Basin on pages 54 and 55. On the "Exploring the West" map you began in chapter 2, find and label the Great Basin. Then, find and label Fremont Peak. Its map coordinates are 43°05'N 109°38'W.

WORKING WITH PRIMARY SOURCES

Reread the "Double Vision: Two Ways to Say It" feature on page 57 of your book. Answer the following questions in your history journal.

1. What emotions do you think are shown in Frémont's descriptions of his expeditions?

2. What emotions do Preuss's words show?

Write your thoughts in your history journal. Then, imagine you are a reporter during the U.S. Civil War. Your assignment: write a profile of John C. Frémont, highlighting his accomplishments during the first 50 years of his life.

TEXAS: TEMPTING AND BEAUTIFUL

SUMMARY *American settlers moved into Texas in the 1820s and 1830s. In 1836 they threw off Mexican rule and established an independent republic.*

ACCESS

Texas experienced great political changes in the first half of the 1800s. The sequence of events chart (model on page 9 of this book) can help you understand these rapid changes. In the first box, write "Spain rules Texas." Fill in the boxes that follow as you connect events. The final box should contain an event that occurred in 1845.

WORD BANK   presidio   hacienda   vaquero

Choose words from the word bank to complete the sentences.

1. The _____ worked all day at the _____ tending cattle.

2. Soldiers at the _____ decided to investigate what was causing the disturbance.

WITH A PARENT OR PARTNER

The words in the word bank are Spanish words. Many Spanish words are commonly used by English speakers. In your journal, list as many Spanish words that have come into the English language as you can think of in one minute. For extra fun, ask a parent or partner to make a list too. Then compare lists by reading aloud. Look up any unfamiliar words in a dictionary.

CRITICAL THINKING   CLASSIFICATION

Texas had four different governments between 1800 and 1850. Make a chart with four columns in your history journal. Label the columns *Spain*, *Mexico*, *Republic of Texas*, and *United States*. Write each of the phrases below in the correct column.

Sam Houston was president   missions were built to convert Indians

Santa Anna takes control   explorers search for cities of gold

Texans consider secession   Andrew Jackson says no to his old friend

a constitution is written in 1824   rebels attack San Antonio

Sam Houston was governor   presidios protect the missions

a new flag with one lone star   Sam Houston was a senator

MAP

Study the map of the Texas War for Independence on page 63. Then, in the back of this study guide, find the blank relief map of the western U.S. Title it *Texas and the War with Mexico*. Add the *Republic of Texas* and *Disputed Area* to the legend and label them on the map. Label the following on the map:

San Antonio   Alamo

Gonzales   San Jacinto

Goliad   Santa Fe

Rio Grande

WORKING WITH PRIMARY SOURCES   IN YOUR OWN WORDS

Reread the quote in italics from Davy Crockett on page 60 of your textbook. Rewrite it in your history journal in your own words.

FIGHTING OVER A BORDER

SUMMARY *A border dispute led to war between the U.S. and Mexico. American forces prevailed in the conflict and the U.S. acquired a large section of Mexican territory.*

ACCESS

Texas was an independent republic from 1836 to 1845. Only a year after Texas joined the Union, war broke out between the U.S. and Mexico. Do you think Texas joining the Union increased tensions between America and Mexico? Chapter 11 discusses the Mexican War. In your history journal, copy the "K-W-L" chart on page 8. In the first column, list everything you know about the war (if you don't know anything, that's okay.) Then, skim through the chapter and look at illustrations and maps. Fill in the second column with questions and things you want to know about the war. Fill in the third column with facts that you learn about the Mexican War as you read the chapter.

WORD BANK   war hawk   aggression

Choose a word from the word bank to complete the sentence. One word is not used.

1. The senator's many speeches supporting the war earned him a reputation as a _____.

Look up in a dictionary the word that you did not use. Write that word in a sentence.

MAP

Study the map on page 66 of your textbook. Answer the following in your history journal.

1. What do the red dotted lines represent?

2. What do you think the yellow stars on the map represent?

3. After the Mexican War ended, which two rivers formed the U.S.-Mexican border?

4. List four current U.S. states that were once part of Mexico.

On the "Texas and the War with Mexico" map you began in chapter 10, add "Ceded by Mexico" to the Legend and mark the boundary on the map. Label the following on the map:

San Diego	Los Angeles
Monterey	San Francisco
Santa Fe	Gila River

WORKING WITH PRIMARY SOURCES

Frederick Douglass wrote the following words about the Mexican War.

> In our judgment, those who have all along been loudly in favor of . . . the war, and heralding its bloody triumphs with apparent rapture . . . have succeeded in robbing Mexico of her territory. . . . We are not the people to rejoice; we ought rather blush and hang our heads for shame.

1. Whom do you think Douglass is addressing?

2. What does Douglass believe the Americans are doing to Mexico?

3. According to Douglass, how should Americans feel about the war?

Record your responses in your history journal.

WRITING

Imagine that the year is 1847. You have been reading newspapers to follow the progress of the Mexican War. Write a poem or song expressing your feelings about the war.

CHAPTER 12

THERE'S GOLD IN THEM HILLS

SUMMARY *Gold was discovered in California in 1848. The following year thousands of people flooded into the territory hoping to strike it rich.*

ACCESS   The discovery of gold in California brought enormous changes to the territory. In your history journal, label one page *Gold in California*. Make two columns, one labeled *positives*, the other labeled *negatives*. Fill in the columns as you read and learn about how the discovery of gold affected life in California.

WORD BANK   nativism   Know-Nothings   prospector   forty-niner

Choose words from the word bank to complete the sentences.

1. The _____ who traveled to California was also called a _____.

2. Motivated by _____, the _____ sought to keep immigrants out of the country.

WORD PLAY   Look up the word *nativism* in a dictionary. Write that word in a sentence.

_____

How did *nativists* feel about Native Americans? _____

Do you see any irony in the term *nativist*? (Look up "irony" in the dictionary if it's unfamiliar.)

_____

CRITICAL THINKING   CAUSE AND EFFECT

Match the effect in the left column with the correct cause in the right column. Write them as sentences connected with the word *because*.

1. The population of California increased rapidly   a.   it was the cheapest way to travel to the state.

2. James Marshall died a poor man   b.   demand was high.

3. Most people traveled overland to California   c.   he never profited from his gold discovery.

4. Chinese people were attacked   d.   gold had been discovered in the state.

5. Prices were high in California   e.   few women lived in California.

6. Men traveled for miles to hear a female voice   f.   nativists blamed immigrants for their troubles.

MAP   On the "Exploring the West" map you began in chapter 2, find and label the location of Sutter's Mill. Its map coordinates are 38°48'N 120°53'W.

WORKING WITH PRIMARY SOURCES

Louisa Clappe lived at a mining camp in California. She wrote:

> Gold mining is nature's great lottery scheme. A man may work in a claim for many months, and be poorer at the end of the time than when he commenced; or he may take out thousands in a few hours. It is a mere matter of chance.

Think about the comparison between gold mining in 1849 to the lottery games of today. Do you think it's accurate? Write about some similatiries and differences in your history journal. Then imagine the year is 1850. You have just returned to the East Coast after spending the past two years in California. A friend informs you that he intends to move to California to mine for gold. Write a letter to your friend reacting to his decision.

CHAPTER 13

CLIPPER SHIPS AND PONY EXPRESS

SUMMARY *New fast clipper ships reduced the time it took to travel overseas from the East Coast to the West Coast. The Pony Express and the telegraph increased the speed of communications in North America.*

ACCESS In 1849 thousands of people poured into California. The growing population on the West Coast created a need for faster ways to travel and communicate. The resulting improvements would have lasting effects on the nation's development. Timelines help us see how events in history are connected. As you read the chapter, write an important event that happened during each year listed below.

1832   1844   1850   1858   1860

WORD BANK   Levis   clipper ship   Pony Express   telegraph

Choose words from the word bank to complete the sentences.

1. The Flying Cloud, a _____ sailed from Boston to San Francisco in less than three months.

2. _____ became popular with miners, who needed sturdy pants.

3. Thanks to Samuel Morse, people could use a _____ to send messages instantly over long distances.

4. The galloping horses of the _____ could deliver a letter from Missouri to California in only 10 days.

MAP Study the map on page 81 of your textbook. Answer the following in your history journal.

1. What was the easternmost point on the Pony Express route?

2. What was the highest point on the Pony Express route?

3. If you sent a letter from Salt Lake City to Sacramento, which direction would the Pony Express riders travel to deliver your letter?

4. What was the lowest point on the Pony Express route?

5. At the time it was active, the Pony Express went through which three U.S. states?

On the "Exploring the West" map you began in chapter 2, add "The Pony Express" to the legend and mark the route on the map. Label the following on the map:

St Joseph   Sacramento

Carson City   Great Salt Lake

Lake Tahoe

COMPREHENSION In your history journal, explain why each of the following individuals was important to people living in California.

Levi Strauss   a clipper ship captain   Samuel F.B. Morse   a Pony Express rider   Joseph Henry

WORKING WITH PRIMARY SOURCES The following is from a Pony Express recruitment ad:

WANTED: Young skinny wirey fellows, not over 18. Must be expert riders willing to risk death daily. Orphans preferred. Wages $25 per week. Apply, Central Overland Express, Alta Building, Montgomery Street, San Francisco.

1. Why do you think the Pony Express wanted young skinny men?

2. Why do you think the Pony Express preferred orphans?

3. Why do you think young men rode for the Pony Express?

Answer these questions in your history journal.

CHAPTER 14

FLYING BY STAGECOACH

SUMMARY *Stagecoaches carried people and mail between Missouri and California.*

ACCESS

During the 1850s and 1860s, stagecoaches were the fastest way to travel overland across the West. Copy the main idea map from page 8 in your history journal. In the largest circle, write *Stagecoaches*. In each of the smaller circles, write one fact that you learn as you read the chapter.

WORD BANK   stagecoach

Look up the word *stagecoach* in a dictionary. Use it in a sentence.

WORD PLAY

The word *stagecoach* is a compound word. Look up the words *stage* and *coach* in a dictionary. Each of the words has multiple definitions. Identify the definition for each word that best fits with the word *stagecoach*. Write two sentences, one using the word *stage*, and one using the word *coach*.

WORKING WITH PRIMARY SOURCES

Fitz Hugh Ludlow described his experience riding in a stagecoach.

> It was . . . like being in an armchair, and sentenced not to get out of it from Missouri to California . . . . The back cushions of the wagon were stuffed as hard as cricket-balls, and the seat might have been the flat side of a bat. I tried fastening my head in a corner by a pocket-handkerchief sling; but just as unconsciousness arrived, the head was sure to slip out, and, in despair, I finally gave over trying to do anything with it.

Write answers to these questions in your history journal.

1. To what did Ludlow compare his seat?

2. What did Ludlow seek to do while traveling?

3. How successful was he at achieving his goal?

4. Why does he use the word "sentenced?" To what is he comparing his trip?

WRITING

Write a letter to a friend describing the most uncomfortable trip you ever had. Where were you going? Was the trip worth it? Illustrate it with your own pictures or cartoons.

ARITHMETIC AT SEA

SUMMARY *Overseas trade brought great wealth to New England's merchants. Nathaniel Bowditch's discoveries in mathematics and navigation allowed American sailors to travel more quickly on the world's oceans.*

ACCESS

Nathanial Bowditch was a remarkable man who improved oceanic navigation. In your history journal, copy the main idea map graphic organizer from page 8. In the largest circle put *Bowditch*. In the smaller circles write facts that you learn about Bowditch as you read the chapter.

WORD BANK   tar   latitude   longitude   navigator

Choose words from the word bank to complete the sentences. One word is used twice.

1. The success of the trading voyage depended upon the skill of the ship's _____.

2. Sailors brought along buckets of _____ to _____ down the ropes.

3. Large waves tossed the ship about, making it difficult for the captain to figure the exact _____ and

_____ of his vessel.

WORD PLAY

Look up the word *navigator* in a dictionary. In five minutes, write down anything you can think of that requires a navigator. Ask a parent or partner to do the same. Then compare your lists.

CRITICAL THINKING   MAKING INFERENCES

Use the information in Chapter 15 to evaluate the following inferences. Place a check in the blank next to each inference that is valid.

_____ 1. A typical New England merchant ship contained many teenage sailors.

_____ 2. Every person in Salem, Massachusetts, was rich.

_____ 3. Pepper was highly valued in Europe.

_____ 4. Nathaniel Bowditch was largely forgotten after his death.

_____ 5. Sailors in Europe read *The New American Practical Navigator*.

_____ 6. Nathaniel Bowditch jealously guarded the discoveries he made.

_____ 7. Most Americans in 1796 had never seen an elephant.

_____ 8. Navigation errors caused many shipwrecks.

WORKING WITH PRIMARY SOURCES

Read Harriet Martineau's description of Salem on page 90. Answer the questions using complete sentences in your history journal.

1. What does Martineau find noteworthy about the town?

2. Do you believe Martineau's opinion of the city was positive or negative? Explain your answer.

WRITING

Imagine that you are a teacher writing a report card for 10-year-old Nathaniel Bowditch. Begin like this: "Nathaniel loves to learn." Continue the report in your history journal.

THAR SHE BLOWS!

SUMMARY *Whaling was a dangerous but profitable profession for New England sailors.*

ACCESS

Chapter 16 places you on the deck of a nineteenth century whaling ship. You are part of a crew that sails around the world hunting for whales. The sequence of events chart on page 9 will help you understand the different stages of a whale hunt. In the first box, write *Thar she blows!* or *A whale is spotted*. Fill in the following boxes with the succession of events that occur during a whale hunt.

WORD BANK   ambergris   trying   Nantucket sleigh ride

Choose words from the word bank to complete the sentences.

1. After being harpooned, the whale took the sailors on what was called a _____.

2. Whales were valued for their spermaceti and their _____.

3. After finishing the _____ process, the crew stored the barrels of whale oil in the lower deck.

MAP

Look at the map on page 98. Answer the questions in your history journal.

1. What do the red lines and red arrows on the map represent?

2. How long was the New Bedford whaler out at sea?

3. The whaling ship sailed through which oceans?

4. In which ocean did the whaler travel the greatest distance?

WORKING WITH PRIMARY SOURCES

Reread Eliza Azelia Williams's journal entry on page 99 of your book. Answer the questions in your history journal.

1. Where is the whale that Williams observed?

2. What are the crew members doing to the whale?

3. How does Williams seem to be affected by the experience of observing the whale?

WRITING

On page 101, the author describes whaling as "brutal, destructive, useful, profitable, wasteful, and exciting." Write a few sentences about how whaling deserves to be called each of those adjectives.

CHAPTER 17
A JAPANESE BOY IN AMERICA

SUMMARY *Nakahama Manjiro was a Japanese boy who was brought to the United States to live with a whaling ship captain's family. Manjiro later returned to Japan and advised the shogun after Commodore Matthew Perry sought to establish a U.S.-Japanese trade agreement.*

ACCESS

In Chapter 17 you will learn about a Japanese boy who came to live in America. Japan and the United States were very different in the 1800s, though the nations had certain similarities. In your history journal, make a Venn diagram like the one on page 9. Label one circle *Japan* and the other *United States*. As you read, fill in the diagram with similarities and differences

WORD BANK   haiku   feudal system   serf   Samurai

Choose words from the word bank to complete the sentences.

1. The _____ worked hard every day but his landlord was never impressed.

2. Americans enjoyed reading _____ that had been translated into English.

3. An emperor and a shogun ruled at the top of Japan's _____.

4. _____ in Japan were similar to knights in Europe.

WORD PLAY

The word *haiku* is Japanese in origin. Choose two other words commonly used by English speakers that have Japanese origins (use a dictionary if you need help). In your history journal, write sentences using each of the words you selected.

CRITICAL THINKING   SEQUENCE OF EVENTS

The sentences below describe events that you learned about in Chapter 17. Put them in order by writing numbers in the blanks next to each event. Write "1" next to the earliest event.

_____ Manjiro earns $600 working in the goldfields of California.

_____ A 15-year-old boy becomes emperor of Japan.

_____ Manjiro and his friends are stranded on an island.

_____ Commodore Matthew Perry sails to Japan for the first time.

_____ Captain Whitfield invites Manjiro to live with him in Massachusetts.

_____ Manjiro accompanies the first Japanese mission to the United States.

_____ Japan agrees to end its isolation.

WORKING WITH PRIMARY SOURCES

The Japanese Decree of Exclusion stated:

> So long as the sun shall warm the earth, let no Christian dare to come to Japan. . . . If he violate this command, [he] shall pay for it with his head.

Answer the questions in your history journal. Use complete sentences.

1. How did the Japanese feel about foreigners coming to their islands?

2. Why do you think they felt this way at this time?

3. Was the Decree accurate in its statement? Why or why not?

WRITING

Study the example of haiku on page 102. In your journal, write a haiku Nakahama Manjiro might have written while marooned on a deserted island at see for six months.

CHAPTER 18

CITIES AND PROGRESS

SUMMARY *Cities grew in size and number in the 1800s, as America slowly became an urban nation.*

ACCESS

America's growing cities in the 1800s were exciting places of opportunity and technological advances just like today. But life in 19th century cities was also very unlike modern cities. In your history journal, copy the Venn diagram chart from page 9. Label one circle *Modern Cities* and the other *Cities in the 1800s*. As you read the chapter, think of ways cities now and then are both similar and different. Fill in your diagram with what you have learned.

WORD BANK   technology   know-how   water closet   tenement

Choose words from the word bank to complete the sentences.

1. Before the _____ was installed at the house, family members had to use an outhouse.

2. Indoor plumbing was just one example of how _____ changed people's lives in the 1800s.

3. People living in a _____ endured overcrowding and unsafe conditions.

4. Europeans admired Americans for their _____, or ability to make things.

TIMELINE

Copy the timeline graphic organizer on page 9 of this guide in your history journal. Start with 1790 and end with 1860. Divide up the space in ten-year sections. Then fill in information from the book that shows big American changes during that time.

WORKING WITH PRIMARY SOURCES

Reread the lines from Walt Whitman's "Song of Myself," below:

This is the city and I am one of the citizens,
Whatever interests the rest interests me, politics, wars, markets,
    newspapers, schools,
The mayor and councils, banks, tariffs, steamships, factories,
    stocks, real estate and personal estate.

Use complete sentences to answer the questions in your history journal.

1. What does Whitman mean when he writes "Whatever interests the rest interests me?"

2. Which items on Whitman's list still interests people today?

3. If Whitman were writing today, what are three items he might add to his list?

WRITING

Your textbook states:

America's land was so vast that much of it was still unmapped. That added to its allure.

Look up "allure" in a dictionary. In your history journal, write about something you think is alluring.

A LAND OF MOVERS

SUMMARY *In the early 1800s, waves of American settlers moved into the Northwest Territory, where they built farms, towns, schools, and businesses.*

ACCESS

Chapter 19 places you in the role of Jacob, a boy who lived in Indiana. The text describes his life experiences from boyhood to his adult years. In your history journal, copy the sequence of events chart on page 9. In the first box, write "Jacob is born the year his family moves to Indiana." Fill in the boxes that follow with the major events in Jacob's life.

WORD BANK   businessman

1. Look up the word *businessman* in the dictionary. Use it in a sentence.

_____

2. Why does the author say *businessman* is a *new* word?

_____

WITH A PARENT OR PARTNER

In one minute, write all the words or terms you can think of that start with business (you may include two-word terms). Ask a parent or partner to do the same. Then read your lists to each other. Use a dictionary to look up any words either of you doesn't know.

CRITICAL THINKING   COMPARE AND CONTRAST

In this chapter, you not only learn about Jacob, but also his friend Ida. The phrases below describe Jacob and Ida. In your history journal, copy the Venn diagram on page 9. Write *Jacob* above one circle and *Ida* above the other circle. The phrases that apply to only one person go in that person's circle. The phrases that apply to both go in the area where the two circles connect.

born into slavery	moved to Indiana with family
became a state senator	feared being kidnapped
worked in father's store	attended school
lived in Mississippi	proud to be an American
father was born in Germany	had a friend named Ohiyesa

WORKING WITH PRIMARY SOURCES

Reread the "Many Hands" sidebar feature on page 115 of your textbook.

Answer the questions in your history journal. Use complete sentences.

1. What work did men do to help their neighbors?
2. What work did women do to help their neighbors?
3. Why do you think people were so willing to get together and help a neighbor with a project?

WRITING

Imagine that Jacob and Ohiyesa had a chance meeting after they were both adults. In your journal, write a story, including dialogue, describing this meeting.

WORKIN' ON THE RAILROAD

SUMMARY *In 1854 a railroad line from the East Coast reached the Mississippi River. Overcoming opposition from steamboat operators, the railroad crossed the Mississippi two years later.*

ACCESS

In 1820 there were only 60 steamboats on the Mississippi River. By 1860, a thousand steamboats sailed the river. Railroads expanded at a similar pace. Over 30,000 miles of track had been laid by 1860. In some places, railroads and steamboats were competitors. They tried to stop each other. Look at the U.S. political map in the Atlas section at the back of the book. Where in the country do you think steamboat companies and railroad companies were most likely to come into conflict? Write your ideas in your history journal. Then, divide a page in your history journal into two columns. Label one column *Railroads* and the other column *Steamboats*. As you read the chapter, write facts that you learn about railroads and steamboats in their respective columns.

WORD BANK   commerce

Look up the word *commerce* in a dictionary. Find the sentence on page 119 in which the word appears. Rewrite the sentence using the definition of the word. _____

_____

WORD PLAY   Think of two synonyms for the word *commerce* (use a thesaurus if you need help). Write two sentences—one for each of these words.

_____

_____

CRITICAL THINKING   CAUSE AND EFFECT

In your history journal, copy the cause and effect chart from page 9. Write an effect for each cause below.

1. The *Effie Afton* ran into a railroad bridge, so . . .

2. Railroad men needed a good lawyer, so . . .

3. Railroad builders wanted to reach the West, so . . .

4. The first train reached Rock Island in 1854, so . . .

5. The train tracks followed a northern route, so . . .

6. Boilers on trains and steamboats often blew up, so . . .

WORKING WITH PRIMARY SOURCES

Study the Chicago and Rock Island Rail Road advertisement on page 117 of your textbook.

Answer the questions in your history journal. Use complete sentences.

1. What are two advantages that the railroad company promises to its passengers?

2. How many trains leave Chicago each day?

3. Who do you think would be most interested in this advertisement?

WRITING

Suppose you are a lawyer defending the railroad company that is being sued by the owner of the *Effie Afton*. In your history journal, write a legal argument defending the railroad company's right to build bridges across the Mississippi River. Brainstorm defense strategies with a friend or some classmates if you can.

"SHE WISHES TO ORNAMENT THEIR MINDS"

SUMMARY *In the nineteenth century, several reformers worked to expand educational opportunities in America.*

ACCESS

You will learn about several important reformers and educators in this chapter. Copy the main idea map from page 8. In the largest circle, write *Reformers and Educators*. In each of the smaller circles, write the name of a person who advanced education in America. Add smaller circles noting important accomplishments.

WORD BANK   universal education   temperance

Choose words from the word bank to complete the sentences.

1. Speakers promoting _____ traveled throughout the country warning people about the evils of alcohol.

2. George Washington believed the U.S. should adopt a plan of _____.

WORD PLAY

The root word of temperance is temper. Look up the word temper in a dictionary. You will find that there are several definitions of the word. Which of the definitions fits best with the word temperance? Using this definition, write a sentence with the word temper.

CRITICAL THINKING   CLASSIFICATION

In the nineteenth century many educational institutions were open to students of only one gender. Make a chart with three columns in your history journal. Label the columns *Male Students*, *Female Students*, and *Both*. Write the name of each of the institutions below in the correct column.

Mt. Holyoke	Tapping Reeve Law School
Bowdoin	Litchfield Female Academy
Oberlin College	Harvard
Troy Female Seminary	Dartmouth
Wesleyan College (Macon, Georgia)	Brown

WORKING WITH PRIMARY SOURCES

According to George Washington, "Knowledge is, in every country, the surest basis of public happiness." Thomas Jefferson wrote, "If a nation expects to be ignorant and free, in a state of civilization, it expects what never was and never will be."

1. What are Washington and Jefferson calling for?

2. Do you agree with Washington and Jefferson's statements?

3. Why or why not?

Write your thoughts in your history journal, using complete sentences.

WRITING

Choose one of the people you learned about in Chapter 21. In your history journal, write an essay explaining how he or she advanced education in the United States.

DO GIRLS HAVE BRAINS?

SUMMARY *Several women spoke out against the idea that females were inferior and unable to learn serious academic subjects.*

ACCESS

Divide a page in your history journal into two columns. Label the first column *Then* and the other column *Now*. As you read the chapter, fill in the first column with facts about how girls were treated in America in the 1800s. In the second column, note how the situation is different today.

WORD BANK   sanction   rational

Choose words from the word bank to complete the sentences.

1. Despite the protests, the college would not _____ the admission of female students.

2. No _____ person would agree with that narrow-minded policy today.

WITH A PARENT OR PARTNER

Look up the word *sanction* in a dictionary. In your history journal, list as many words as you can think of that have a similar meaning. Ask a parent or partner to also make a list. Compare the words that you each wrote down. Look up any new words that either of you does not know.

CRITICAL THINKING   MAIN IDEA AND SUPPORTING DETAILS

In your history journal, fill in details to support the main ideas from the chapter below.

1. *A woman married to a bad man was not much better off than a slave.*

2. *But even good men were horrified at the idea of a woman standing up and speaking her mind.*

WORKING WITH PRIMARY SOURCES

Reread the selection on page 126 from *Letters on the Equality of the Sexes and the Condition of Women*. Answer the questions in your history journal.

1. According to the Grimké sisters, why did so few women develop their intellectual abilities?

2. What did the Grimké sisters say about working women?

3. What widely accepted idea of their day did the Grimké sisters challenge?

WRITING

Suppose that Sarah and Angelina Grimké could spend a week observing modern America. What do you think they would have to say about gender relations today? In your history journal, write a commentary about American society from the Grimké sisters' perspective.

SENECA FALLS AND THE RIGHTS OF WOMEN

A WOMAN NAMED *TRUTH*

SUMMARY *Determined reformers organized a national movement to win equal rights for women. Sojourner Truth, a former slave, became famous for her determined efforts to promote abolitionism, women's rights, and temperance.*

ACCESS

In Chapters 23 and 24 you will learn about women who led the women's rights movement. In your history journal, copy the "K-W-L" chart on page 8. In the first column, write everything you know about the women's rights movement of the nineteenth century. Then, skim through the chapter and look at illustrations and maps. Fill in the second column with questions and things you want to know about the movement. Go back to this chart after finishing the chapters and write notes in the final column, "What I Learned."

WORD BANK   abolition   bloomers   abolitionist

Choose words from the word bank to complete the sentences.

1. Despite the insults, the ladies were far more comfortable wearing _____ on their walk.

2. Sojourner Truth was an _____ as well as a champion of women's rights.

3. Many women worked to bring about the _____ of slavery.

WORD PLAY

Bloomers are named after Amelia Bloomer, a nineteenth century reformer. In your journal, list as many words in the English language as you can think of that were named after a person (for example, the Venn diagram on page 9 is named after John Venn). Try to think of at least five words. Write a sentence using one of the words below.

CRITICAL THINKING   SUMMARIZING

In your history journal, write a sentence summarizing at least one notable achievement of each of the following women:

Dorothea Dix   Sojourner Truth

Susan B. Anthony   Julia Archibald Holmes

Julia Ward Howe   Lucretia Mott

Elizabeth Cady Stanton

WORKING WITH PRIMARY SOURCES

Sojourner Truth spoke the following words at a women's rights convention in 1851:

> A'n't I a woman? Look at me. Look at my arm. I have ploughed, and planted, and gathered into barns, and no man could head me! And a'n't I a woman? I could work as much and eat as much as a man—when I could get it—and bear the lash as well! And a'n't I a woman? I have borne thirteen children, and seen most all sold off to slavery, and when I cried out with my mother's grief, none but Jesus heard me! And a'n't I a woman?

Explain in your journal, in your own words, the point Sojourner Truth is making with this statement.

WRITING

Words were among the most important weapons women used in their battle for equal rights. Use a library or media center to find an additional quote from a reformer mentioned in your book, such as Margaret Fuller. In your history journal, explain why the quote you selected was important to the women's rights movement.

LIFE IN THE MILLS

SUMMARY *Industrialization forced many workers, including children, to toil in unsafe working conditions. Excessive heat and noise made steel mills especially brutal places to work.*

ACCESS

The Industrial Revolution started in Great Britain in the late 1700s. It soon spread to the United States, transforming the American economy. Though industrialization brought benefits, it created hardships for many people. In your history journal, make a two-column chart. Label one column *Benefits of Industralization* and the other *Drawbacks of Industrialization*. As you read the chapter, make notes in each column.

WORD BANK   labor union   strike

Choose words from the word bank to complete the sentence.

After failing to reach a wage agreement with the factory owners, the members of the _____ voted to go

on _____.

WITH A PARENT OR PARTNER

There are many labor unions in America today. Some have been around for many years. In five minutes, list as many labor unions as you can think of. Ask a parent or family member to make a list, too. Then, compare and discuss your lists. Brainstorm the advantages of belonging to a labor union in the 1800's and today. Are there any disadvantages?

WORKING WITH PRIMARY SOURCES

Reread the description of Wheeling, Virginia on pages 139 and 140. Then read Rebecca Harding's description of conditions at a Wheeling iron mill on page 141. In your history journal, draw or collage a picture based on Rebecca Harding's descriptions.

WRITING

Imagine you are a child worker for one of Wheeling's mills or mines. In your history journal, describe a typical day at work. How do you feel about your job? What kind of working conditions do you have?

HISTORY JOURNAL

Don't forget to share your history journal with your classmates, and ask if you can see what their journals look like. You might be surprised—and get some new ideas.

CHAPTER 26

WORKING WOMEN AND CHILDREN

SUMMARY *In America many women and children took jobs in factories, where they labored for long hours in harsh working conditions.*

ACCESS

The Industrial Revolution increased the pace of work. Factories had strict rules about when workers had to be on the job, and how much they had to produce. Many workers struggled to keep pace with the relentless machines. To organize information about the American workforce in the nineteenth century, use the outline graphic organizer on page 8. As you read the chapter, identify two or more main ideas that relate to American workers (for example *Woman Wage Earners* and *Children Wage Earners*). Write these down on the "Main Idea" lines of the outline. Fill in details about each main idea in the lines below.

WORD BANK   cooper   textile mill

Choose words from the word bank to complete the sentences.

1. Yesterday, father bought three barrels from the _____.

2. Most of the girls in town work at the _____ making cloth.

WORD PLAY

Look up the word cooper in a dictionary. What part of speech is it? Write one sentence using cooper as a noun, and another sentence using cooper (or a form of the word) as a verb.

_____

_____

CRITICAL THINKING   DRAWING CONCLUSIONS

Place a check mark in the blanks in front of all the sentences that are valid conclusions that can be drawn from the information in the chapter.

_____ 1. Factory owners treated their male and female employees equally.

_____ 2. Many children in America had to work to help support their families.

_____ 3. Textile mills were noisy places.

_____ 4. Most children would rather work in a factory than go to school.

_____ 5. There were few government restrictions on child labor in the mid-1800s.

_____ 6. Factory workers in the mid-1800s received excellent health benefits.

_____ 7. Children were taught to operate machines in factories.

_____ 8. Herman Melville was a factory owner.

WRITING

Reread Mary Paul's letter to her father on page 144. Why do you think Mary said she would advise other girls to come to Lowell? Write your thoughts in your history journal. Then, imagine you had been assigned by the President of the United States to investigate conditions at the nation's factories. You spend several months touring factories and mills. What changes would you recommend? Write your report in your history journal.

AMERICAN WRITERS

MR. THOREAU—AT HOME WITH THE WORLD

SUMMARY *A group of New England writers produced a body of literature that was distinctly American. One of these writers was Henry David Thoreau, who promoted self-honesty and nonviolent resistance of injustice.*

ACCESS

Romanticism was an intellectual movement that started in Europe. Romantics emphasized intuition and emotion as sources of truth. They also believed the individual had unlimited potential. Romanticism was a major influence on American writers in the nineteenth century. Copy the main idea map from page 8. In the largest circle, write *American Literature*. In each of the smaller circles, write the name of one writer you learn about as you read the chapter. Write at least two details about each writer.

WORD BANK   sage   civil disobedience   passive resistance   oxymoron

Choose words from the word bank to complete the sentences.

1. Henry David Thoreau promoted _____ to inspire people to oppose governmental injustice.

2. _____ sounds like an _____, but it is actually an effective way to fight oppression.

3. Many of his readers considered Ralph Waldo Emerson to be a _____.

WITH A PARENT OR PARTNER

Look up the word oxymoron in a dictionary. In five minutes list as many oxymora as you can think of (for example, jumbo shrimp). For extra fun, ask a parent or partner to do the same. Then read your lists to each other. Look up any unfamiliar terms.

CRITICAL THINKING   COMPARE AND CONTRAST

The phrases below describe Ralph Waldo Emerson and Henry David Thoreau. In your history journal, copy the Venn diagram on page 9. Write *Emerson* above one circle and *Thoreau* above the other circle. The phrases that apply to only one person go in that person's circle. The phrases that apply to both go in the area where the two circles connect.

student at Harvard	lived in a cabin on the edge of Walden Pond
wrote an essay titled *Civil Disobedience*	known as the "Sage of Concord"
wrote a poem called "Fable"	loved nature
drew people to himself	jailed for not paying taxes

WORKING WITH PRIMARY SOURCES

Henry David Thoreau wrote:

> Be a Columbus to whole new continents and worlds within you. . . . Explore the private sea, the Atlantic and Pacific Ocean of one's being.

In your history journal, write what you think this passage means. Write about how you could — or would like to — follow Thoreau's advice.

MELVILLE AND COMPANY

SUMMARY *In the mid-1800s, a diverse group of writers captured the public's imagination by writing novels, stories, and poems about the American experience.*

ACCESS

Chapter 29 will introduce you to many great American writers. As you read, write down the name of each writer you learn about in the chapter. Next to each name, write at least one work that he or she wrote. Write at least two adjectives that could describe the writer and at least two more that could describe the writer's work.

WORD BANK   reverie   barbarous   forecastle   tall tale

Choose words from the word bank to complete the sentences.

1. Sailors gathered in the ship's _____ to discuss their new work assignments.

2. The passengers feared they would fall into the hands of a _____ people.

3. Lost in a _____, the student did not hear the professor's question.

4. Mike Fink's accomplishments became the subject of a _____.

WORD PLAY

The prefix *fore-* has more than one meaning. In the word *forecastle*, the prefix means the "front or forward part of." List three other words that include the prefix *fore-* with that meaning. Write a sentence using each of the words in your history journal.

WORKING WITH PRIMARY SOURCES

Reread the passage from Herman Melville's *White Jacket* on page 152 of your textbook.

Answer the questions in your history journal.

1. How does Melville describe life on land (terra firma)?

2. How does Melville describe life on the sea?

3. What animal does Melville compare to the sea?

WRITING

In your history journal, write a tall tale about an actual person you know. You may wish to read one of the tall tales mentioned on page 155 of your textbook for ideas on what to write. Don't be afraid to exaggerate — that's the point of a tall tale. Use your imagination and have fun with this assignment.

IF A POET WRITES YOU A LETTER, PAY ATTENTION

SUMMARY *Emily Dickinson and Walt Whitman wrote beautiful poetry that was unlike anything that had been written before. Though controversial in their day, Dickinson and Whitman are now regarded as two of America's greatest poets.*

ACCESS

Before Emily Dickinson and Walt Whitman, poets were expected to write in a certain style. Violating the accepted rules of poetry was condemned by literary "experts." In this chapter you will learn about two poets who broke with tradition to create their own original style. Make a two column chart in your history journal. Write *Whitman* at the top of one column and *Dickinson* at the top of the other column. As you read the chapter, make notes about the poetic styles of each writer.

WORD BANK   Paumanok

Find the sentence on page 156 that uses the word in the word bank. Read the following sentence in the textbook to learn the definition of the word. Write a sentence using the word *Paumanok*.

WITH A PARENT OR PARTNER

The English language includes many words that have Native American origins (e.g. maize). In your history journal, make a list of Native American words that are commonly used by English speakers. Try to think of at least 10 words. Ask a parent or partner to make a list as well. Compare your lists. Look up any words that either of you does not know.

CRITICAL THINKING   COMPARE AND CONTRAST

The phrases below describe Emily Dickinson and Walt Whitman. Copy the Venn diagram on page 9. Write Dickinson above one circle and Whitman above the other circle. The phrases that apply to only one person go in that person's circle. The phrases that apply to both go in the area where the two circles connect.

poems not-well received at first

lived in Brooklyn

used an easy, staccato style

loved to use big fancy words

ignored established rules of meter and rhyme

grandfather helped establish Amherst College

wrote with an original rhythm and voice

encouraged by Thomas Wentworth Higginson

poems are numbered, since they didn't have titles

celebrated life in poetry

WRITING

Select one of the poems by Dickinson or Whitman that is included in this chapter. In your journal, write a commentary on the poem that answers the following questions:

1. What is the theme of the poem? (Some popular poetic themes include life, death, love, nature, progress, and freedom — but there are many others.)

2. What emotions does the poem invoke?

3. What does the poem inspire you to think about?

Then, write your own original poem in the style of the poet you chose.

PAINTER OF BIRDS AND PAINTER OF INDIANS

SUMMARY *John James Audubon and George Catlin were two of the most talented painters in America in the first half of the nineteenth century.*

ACCESS

Before reading the chapter, flip through the pages and look at the paintings. Read the captions. Make a two-column chart in your history journal. Label one column *John Jacob Audubon* and one *George Catlin*. For each artist, write a few first impressions about what they painted and their artistic styles. When you've finished the chapter, go back and add details you think are important.

WORD BANK   engraving   ornithologist

Choose words from the word bank to complete the sentences.

1. John met an _____, who told him about several different types of birds.

2. In the 1800s, it took a long time to produce a color _____.

WORD PLAY

The suffix *-ology* means "the study of." Think of all the words you can that end with *–ology*. Write them down in your history journal and then look up what they mean. Write sentences using two of the words.

WORKING WITH PRIMARY SOURCES

The following quote is from George Catlin.

> I love a people who have always made me welcome to the best they had . . . who are honest without laws . . . who have no poor house. . . who never raised a hand against me or stole my property . . . and oh! how I love a people who don't live for the love of money.

1. Whom is Catlin describing in this passage?

2. What does Catlin believe is superior about the group he describes?

Write your answers in your journal. Then think about Audubon's quote on page 164: "My best friends regard me as a madman." Write about a time when you stuck with something, even though people advised you to quit. Why did you choose to stick with it, even when people advised against it?

WRITING

In your history journal, make a drawing that imitates the style of either John James Audubon or George Catlin.

CHAPTER 32

AMISTAD MEANS FRIENDSHIP

SUMMARY *While out at sea, African slaves rebelled and took control of a Spanish slave ship. After landing in America, the U.S. Supreme Court granted the slaves their freedom.*

ACCESS

In 1808 the U.S. Congress banned the importation of slaves into the country. Britain and Spain also outlawed the foreign slave trade. But slave traders continued to bring African slaves into the Americas. The reason: money. This chapter will tell you about Sengbe Pieh, a key figure in the fight against slavery in America. In your history journal, copy the main idea map from page 8 of this guide. In the largest circle, put *Sengbe Pieh*. In each of the smaller circles, write one fact about Pieh that you learn as you read the chapter.

WORD BANK   barracoon   coffle   Ladino   slaver   mutiny   gag rule

Choose words from the word bank to complete the paragraph. One term is not used at all.

Near his village in Sierra Leone, Sengbe Pieh was surrounded by four armed men. They captured Pieh and several

others. They placed the captives in a _____ and marched them to the African coast. There, the slaves

were held in a _____ for several weeks. After his men had captured enough slaves to fill his ship, the

_____ sailed across the Atlantic. In Cuba, the Spanish gave Pieh the European name Cinque and

labeled him a _____. Cinque was sold and placed on another ship. While out at sea, Cinque led a

_____ and gained control of the ship. It eventually landed on the New England coast. After several

trials, he and the other captives won their freedom.

WORD PLAY

Use a dictionary to learn the meaning of the word or term that you did not use. What are alternative words that could be used to convey the same meaning? Try to think of at least three different examples. Write a sentence using one of the alternative words.

WORKING WITH PRIMARY SOURCES

When arguing before the Supreme Court for the Cinque's and the other slaves' freedom, John Quincy Adams stated:

> I know of no other law that reaches the case of my clients, but the law of Nature and of Nature's God on which our fathers placed our own national existence.

Answer the following questions in your history journal:

1. To whom is Adams referring when he says "our fathers?"

2. How do Adams's words advance the argument that the *Amistad* slaves should be freed?

WRITING

The year is 1841. You are a lawyer who has been hired to represent Cinque and the other slaves aboard the Amistad. In your history journal, write why the slaves should be freed. Brainstorm your ideas with friends or classmates in a small group, if possible.

40   CHAPTER 32

WEBSTER DEFENDS THE UNION

SUMMARY *In 1850 a growing number of southerners wanted to secede from the United States. To keep the Union together, Daniel Webster endorsed Henry Clay's compromise proposal.*

ACCESS

In 1850 three great leaders and speakers had a final say about the future of the United States. Divide a page in your history journal into three columns. Label one column *Henry Clay*. Label the second column *John C. Calhoun*. Label the third column *Daniel Webster*. As you read the chapter, write at least three ideas put forth by each person in his respective column.

WORD BANK   nullify   Unionist   secession   confederacy   fugitive slave law

Choose words from the word bank to complete the paragraph.

John C. Calhoun believed that the United States was a _____ of independent states. He therefore held

that a state had a right to _____ a law it believed to be unconstitutional. Inspired by Calhoun, many

southern leaders believed that _____ was the best way to preserve the institution of slavery. Henry

Clay was a _____ who placed national interests above those of his own state. To keep the Union

together, Clay included a _____ as part of his larger compromise proposal. The plan became known as

the Compromise of 1850.

WORD PLAY

An antonym is a word that means the opposite of another word. Use a thesaurus to find three antonyms of the word nullify. Write sentences in your history journal using each of these words.

CRITICAL THINKING   CAUSE AND EFFECT

Make a T-chart like the one on page 9 of this guide. Label the left column *Causes* and the right column *Effects*. Write down the following causes and fill in their effects from the book.

1. Cassius Marcellus Clay opposed slavery, so . . .
2. Daniel Webster wanted to keep the Union together, so . . .
3. Clay wanted Calhoun's support for his compromise, so . . .
4. The Free Soil Party did not have strong support, so . . .
5. Calhoun was too ill to speak, so . . .
6. Southerners feared that slavery would be outlawed, so . . .

WORKING WITH PRIMARY SOURCES

Reread the excerpt from Daniel Webster's Senate oration (the italicized text on page 179). Answer these questions in your history journal.

1. What does Webster believe is impossible?
2. What does Webster believe will happen if states secede from the Union?
3. According to Webster, what holds the Union together?

WRITING

Imagine you are a reporter in Washington D.C. in 1850. You are covering the debates that are taking place in the U.S. Senate. You may interview Henry Clay, John C. Calhoun, or Daniel Webster. In your history journal, write down five questions you would ask the person you decide to interview. Then write the answers to the questions as you imagine the senator might answer them.

BIG PROBLEMS AND A LITTLE GIANT

SUMMARY *Stephen Douglas promoted the Kansas-Nebraska Act, which repealed the Missouri Compromise. Northerners were furious, and the nation moved closer to civil war.*

ACCESS

Northerners and southerners had several major disagreements in the first half of the nineteenth century. They tried to resolve these disagreements with compromises, such as the Missouri Compromise and the Compromise of 1850. In the 1850s, the two sides grew less interested in compromise. In Chapter 34 you will learn about a series of events that widened the rift between the North and the South. In your history journal, copy the sequence of events chart on page 9. In the first box write *Douglas wants the transcontinental railroad to go through the Louisiana Purchase land.* Fill in other boxes with the events that followed in the 1850s.

WORD BANK

popular sovereignty   border ruffian   free soiler   Bloody Kansas

Choose words from the word bank to complete the sentences.

1. A person who did not want to allow slavery in the Western territories was called a _____.

2. Stephen Douglas promoted _____, the idea that people in the territories should decide whether they want to allow slavery or not.

3. A _____ was a person who crossed the Missouri border to vote for slavery in Kansas.

4. After both pro- and anti-slavery people in Kansas started to fight each other, the territory became known as

    _____.

TIMELINE

In your history journal, copy the timeline graphic organizer on page 9. Include the following dates on your timeline: 1820, 1850, 1853, 1854, and 1856. Read the chapter to learn what happened in each of those years. List each event in the box next to the year in which it happened.

WORKING WITH PRIMARY SOURCES

Reread the passage from Abraham Lincoln's speech on the Kansas-Nebraska Act (the italicized text on page 183). Answer the questions in your history journal, using complete sentences.

1. Does Lincoln support or oppose the Kansas-Nebraska Act?

2. According to Lincoln, what principles cannot co-exist?

3. How does Lincoln believe the Union can be saved?

WRITING

Imagine that you are a U.S. senator in 1854. Stephen Douglas's Kansas-Nebraska bill is being debated in the Senate. It is your turn to speak. In your history journal, write a speech explaining your views on the Kansas-Nebraska bill.

A DREADFUL DECISION

SUMMARY *In the Dred Scott decision the Supreme Court declared that slaves were property and that black people, whether slave or free, had no right to citizenship. The decision paved the way for the Civil War.*

ACCESS

The *Dred Scott* v. *Sanford* case yielded one of the most famous (or infamous) decisions in the history of the Supreme Court. Make a chart with two columns in your history journal. The first column should be called "What I Know." Write everything you already know about the *Dred Scott* decision (If you don't know anything, that's okay). The second column should be called "What I Learned." After you read the chapter, write everything that you have learned about the *Dred Scott* decision and why it was important.

WORD BANK   majority opinion   dissenting opinion

Choose words from the word bank to complete the sentences.

1. The chief justice wrote the _____ in the case.

2. One of the two justices who disagreed wrote the _____.

WORKING WITH PRIMARY SOURCES

The following passage is from Chief Justice Roger Taney's majority opinion in the *Dred Scott* decision. Answer the questions with complete sentences in your history journal.

> The question before us is, whether Negroes compose a portion of the American people and are constituent members of this sovereignty. We think they are not. On the contrary, they are a subordinate and inferior class of beings, who have been subjugated by the dominant race. They can therefore claim none of the rights and privileges which the Constitution provides for citizens of the United States.

1. What does Taney mean by the words "constituent members of this sovereignty?"

2. Whom does Taney consider to be the "dominant race?"

3. Did the *Dred Scott* decision settled the slavery question as President Buchanan had hoped?

WRITING

Look at the political cartoon on page 186 of your book. In your history journal, draw your own political cartoon, criticizing the Supreme Court's decision in the *Dred Scott* case.

CHAPTER 36

FLEEING TO FREEDOM

SUMMARY *Ellen and William Craft devised a clever plan to escape to freedom then spoke out publicly against slavery.*

ACCESS

Ellen and William Craft escaped bondage in the South and found fame in the North. Copy the main idea map from page 8. In the largest circle, write *Ellen and William Craft*. In each of the smaller circles, write one fact that you learn about them as you read the chapter.

WORD BANK   biracial   The Liberator

Choose words from the word bank to complete the sentences.

1. _____ published Elizabeth Cady Stanton's speech to the American Anti-Slavery Society.

2. Having a white father and a black mother, Ellen was _____.

WITH A PARENT OR PARTNER

In five minutes, list all of the English words you can think of that have the same prefix as biracial. Ask a parent or family member or partner to make a list, too. What does the prefix bi- mean?

CRITICAL THINKING   FACT OR OPINION

Make a two-column chart in your journal. Label one column *Fact* and the other column *Opinion*. Write each sentence below from the chapter in the column where it belongs.

1. "She [Ellen Craft] was very intelligent . . ."

2. "She [Ellen] would soon be the best-known black woman of her day."

3. "When Ellen was 11 she was given as a wedding present to her white half-sister."

4. "Less than two years after the Crafts escaped, the Fugitive Slave Law was passed."

5. "Then something fearful happened."

6. "They stayed in a fine hotel . . ."

7. "Then some English merchants sent William to Africa to sell their goods."

8. "They [the Crafts] spent the rest of their lives in the South, teaching and helping others."

WORKING WITH PRIMARY SOURCES

Reread the excerpt from Elizabeth Cady Stanton's speech in the sidebar of page 188 of your textbook. Answer the questions in your history journal.

1. What does Stanton mean by "The badge of degradation is the skin and the sex . . . ?"

2. According to Stanton, which group has the advantages in society?

3. Do you agree with her assessment? (Remember, she gave this speech in 1860.) Give specific examples to support your answer.

WRITING

In your journal, make a list of the things that Ellen Craft did and the qualities about her that you admire. Then write a speech about Ellen that you might deliver at a patriotic celebration. Read it aloud to a parent or partner.

CHAPTER 37

OVER THE RIVER AND UNDERGROUND

SUMMARY *Both white and black Americans organized the Underground Railroad, a system of travel that helped thousands of slaves escape from bondage in the South.*

ACCESS

In your history journal, copy the "K-W-L" chart from page 8. In the first column, write everything you know about the Underground Railroad. Then, skim through the chapter and look at illustrations and maps. Fill in the second column with questions and things you want to know about the Underground Railroad. Go back to this chart after finishing the chapter and write notes in the final column, "What I Learned."

WORD BANK   Underground Railroad   conductor   station   passenger

Choose words from the word bank to complete the sentences.

Levi Coffin was a _____ on the _____. His job was to help each

_____, or runaway slave, travel safely to the next _____ on the route.

MAP

Look at the map on page 193 of your textbook. Answer the questions in your history journal.

1. What do the arrows on the Map represent?

2. The passengers on the Underground Railroad were from which part of the U.S.?

3. List three locations outside of the United States to which the Underground Railroad led.

CRITICAL THINKING   CLASSIFICATION

The Underground Railroad included both passengers and conductors. Some people opposed the Underground Railroad. Make a chart with three columns in your history journal. Label the columns *Conductors*, *Passengers*, and *Opponents*. Each of the people below are mentioned in Chapter 37. Write their names in the correct column. Some individuals may be placed in two columns.

John Price	Dinah	Anetta M. Lane	Levi Coffin
Simeon Bushnell	Shakespeare Boynton	James Grey	Frank
Joshua R. Giddings	Harriet R. Taylor	George Latimer	Jollife Union

WORKING WITH PRIMARY SOURCES

Reread the "Driving That Train" sidebar feature on page 195. Answer the questions in your history journal.

1. What was the "company of 28?"

2. What can you tell about their journey so far?

3. Why do you think Coffin referred to them in a letter as "valuable stock?"

WRITING

Imagine that you are a conductor on the Underground Railroad. In your history journal, write a diary entry telling why you are breaking the law (the Fugitive Slave Law, which was part of the Missouri Compromise), to do this.

SEVEN DECADES

SUMMARY *Seven decades after George Washington's inauguration, the United States faced the greatest challenge to its existence. The crisis of slavery threatened to tear the nation apart.*

ACCESS

The United States was an experiment in democracy. Make a T-chart like the one on page 9 of this book. As you read this chapter, list the evidence that the experiment was going well in one column, and the evidence that the experiment was not going well in the other.

WORD BANK   paradox   unalienable   agitation

Choose words from the word bank to complete the sentences.

According to the Declaration of Independence, a divine creator has given all men certain _____ rights

This created a _____, because many people in America were denied equal rights.

_____ for equality increased in the mid-nineteenth century.

TIMELINE

Review the Chronology of Events on page 199 of your textbook. Copy the timeline graphic organizer into your history journal. Write *1800* at the top of the date line and *1860* at the bottom of the date line. Select six events from the Chronology that you believe were significant. Write these events and the years they occurred on your timeline. Below the description of each event, write a brief explanation of why you selected it for your timeline.

WORKING WITH PRIMARY SOURCES

Frederick Douglass wrote the following words about slavery in 1857.

> Those who profess to favor freedom and yet depreciate agitation, are men who want crops without plowing up the ground, they want rain without thunder and lightning.

1. What is Douglass calling for with this statement?

2. Do you agree with Douglass's assessment? Why or why not?

Write your thoughts in your history journal, using complete sentences.

WRITING

You have learned about many Americans in this textbook. Choose one who you believe made the United States a better place. In your history journal, write an essay explaining why the person you selected was an American hero.

NAME _____

LIBRARY / MEDIA CENTER RESEARCH LOG   DUE DATE _____

What I Need to **Find**

I need to use:

☐ primary
☐ secondary

sources.

Places I **Know** to Look

Brainstorm: Other Sources and Places to Look

WHAT I FOUND

Title/Author/Location (call # or URL)

☐ Book/Periodical
☐ Website
☐ Other

☐ ☐ ☐ ☐ ☐ ☐ ☐
☐ ☐ ☐ ☐ ☐ ☐ ☐
☐ ☐ ☐ ☐ ☐ ☐ ☐

●

●

☐ Primary Source
☐ Secondary Source

☐ ☐ ☐ ☐ ☐ ☐ ☐
☐ ☐ ☐ ☐ ☐ ☐ ☐

How I Found it

☐ Suggestion
☐ Library Catalog
☐ Browsing
☐ Internet Search
☐ Web link

☐ ☐ ☐ ☐ ☐ ☐ ☐
☐ ☐ ☐ ☐ ☐ ☐ ☐
☐ ☐ ☐ ☐ ☐ ☐ ☐
☐ ☐ ☐ ☐ ☐ ☐ ☐
☐ ☐ ☐ ☐ ☐ ☐ ☐

Rate each source from 1 (low) to 4 (high) in the categories below

helpful

relevant

●

LIBRARY/ MEDIA CENTER RESEARCH LOG

NAME _____

DUE DATE _____

What I Need to Find

I need to use:
- [ ] primary
- [ ] secondary

sources.

Brainstorm: Other Sources and Places to Look

Places I **Know** to Look

WHAT I FOUND

Rate each source from 1 (low) to 4 (high) in the categories below

helpful   relevant

How I Found it
- Suggestion
- Library Catalog
- Browsing
- Internet Search
- Web link

- Primary Source
- Secondary Source

Title/Author/Location (call # or URL)

- Book/Periodical
- Website
- Other

LIBRARY / MEDIA CENTER RESEARCH LOG

NAME

DUE DATE

What I Need to **Find**

I need to use:

- [ ] primary
- [ ] secondary

sources.

Places I **Know** to Look

Brainstorm: Other Sources and Places to Look

WHAT I FOUND

Title/Author/Location (call # or URL)

- [ ] Book/Periodical
- [ ] Website
- [ ] Other

- [ ] Primary Source
- [ ] Secondary Source

How I Found it

- [ ] Suggestion
- [ ] Library Catalog
- [ ] Browsing
- [ ] Internet Search
- [ ] Web link

Rate each source from 1 (low) to 4 (high) in the categories below

helpful

relevant

LIBRARY / MEDIA CENTER RESEARCH LOG

NAME _____

DUE DATE _____

What I Need to Find

I need to use:
- [ ] primary
- [ ] secondary

[ ] ____ sources.

Brainstorm: Other Sources and Places to Look

Places I **Know** to Look

WHAT I FOUND

Title/Author/Location (call # or URL)

How I Found it:
- [ ] Suggestion
- [ ] Library Catalog
- [ ] Browsing
- [ ] Internet Search
- [ ] Web link

- [ ] Primary Source
- [ ] Secondary Source

- [ ] Book/Periodical
- [ ] Website
- [ ] Other

Rate each source from 1 (low) to 4 (high) in the categories below

helpful _____   relevant _____

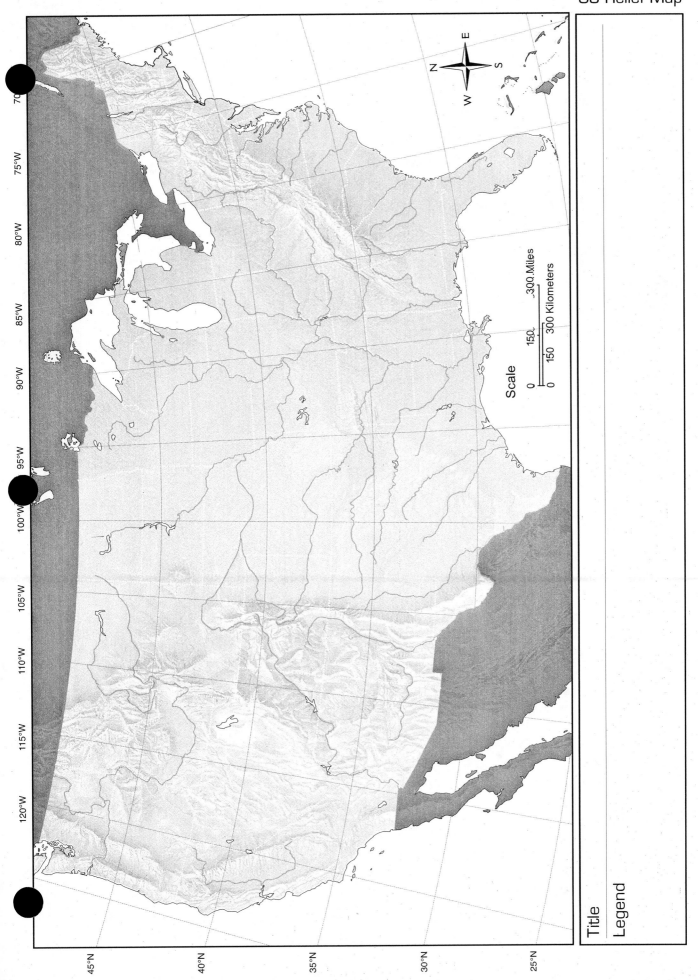

Title

Legend

Scale

300 Miles

300 Kilometers

150

150

0

0

Title

Legend

70°W
75°W
80°W
85°W
90°W
95°W
100°W
105°W
110°W
115°W
120°W

45°N
40°N
35°N
30°N
25°N

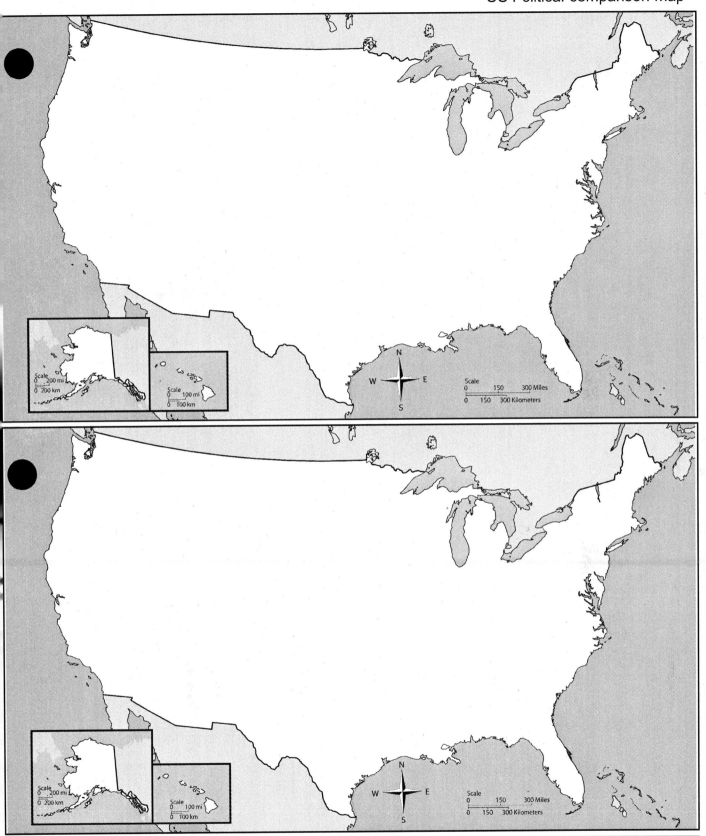

Scale
0   200 mi
0   200 km

Scale
0   100 mi
0   100 km

N
W   E
S

Scale
0   150   300 Miles
0   150   300 Kilometers

Scale
0   200 mi
0   200 km

Scale
0   100 mi
0   100 km

N
W   E
S

Scale
0   150   300 Miles
0   150   300 Kilometers

Title

Legend

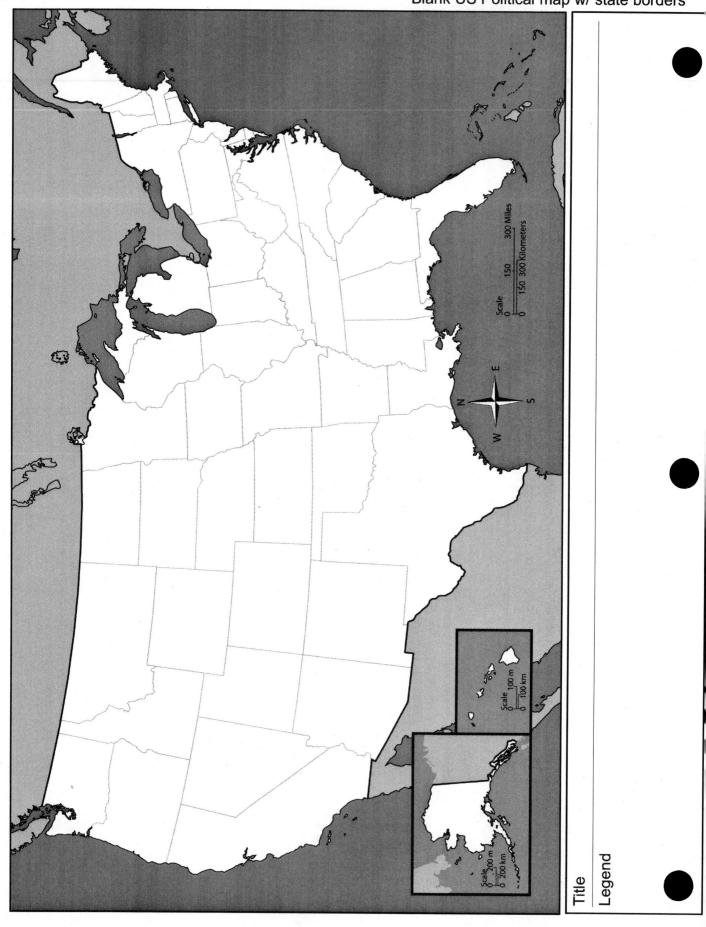

Title

Legend

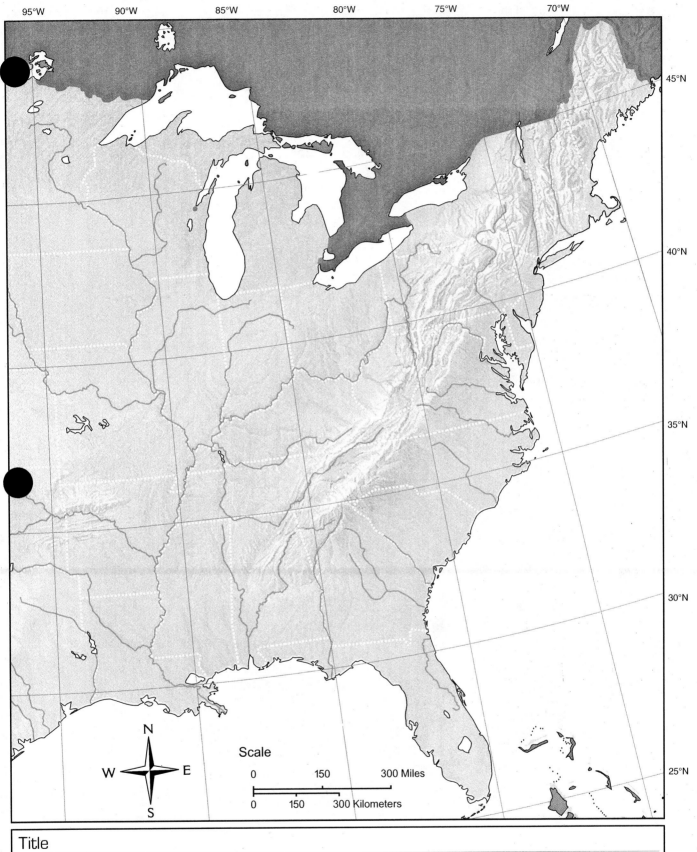

95°W   90°W   85°W   80°W   75°W   70°W

45°N

40°N

35°N

30°N

25°N

N
W   E
S

Scale

0   150   300 Miles

0   150   300 Kilometers

Title

Legend

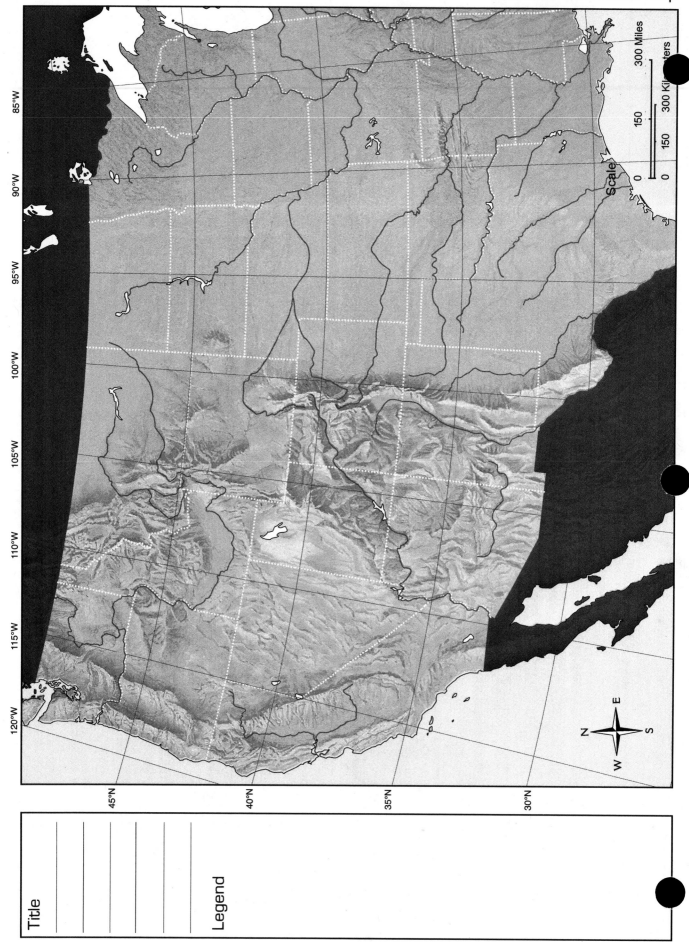

Western US Relief Map

85°W 90°W 95°W 100°W 105°W 110°W 115°W 120°W

45°N 40°N 35°N 30°N

300 Miles
150
300 Kilometers
150
150
0
0
Scale

N
E
W
S

Title

Legend